AUSTRALIAN KANGAROOS AND WALLABIES

Mason Crest Publishers
www.masoncrest.com
Philadelphia

Mason Crest Publishers
370 Reed Road
Broomall, PA 19008
(866) MCP-BOOK (toll free)

First printing

ISBN 1-59084-217-0

Library of Congress Cataloging-in-Publication Data on file at the Library of Congress

First published by Steve Parish Publishing Pty Ltd
PO Box 1058, Archerfield BC
Queensland 4108, Australia
© Copyright Steve Parish Publishing Pty Ltd

Photographic Assistance: Darran Leal

Front Cover & Title Page: Red-Necked Wallabies (photos Steve Parish)

p. 7: Hans & Judy Beste; pp. 9, 10, 25: Stan Breeden; pp. 13, 37, 47: Ian Morris; p. 26: Jiri Lochman; p. 46: Darran Leal

Printed in Jordan

Writing, editing, design, and production by Steve Parish Publishing Pty Ltd, Australia

CONTENTS

▽

Use of Capital Letters for Animal Names in this book
An animal's official common name begins with a capital letter.
Otherwise the name begins with a lowercase letter.

WHAT iS A KANGAROO?

▼ An Eastern Grey Kangaroo hopping.

A kangaroo is a furry animal with big, strong hind legs. When it wants to go fast, the kangaroo hops on its hind legs. It can use its paws to hold things.

Kangaroos have many relatives. Wallabies are small kangaroos. Wallaroos live in rocky places. Bettongs and potoroos are very small.

Kangaroos of all kinds are remarkable animals.

◄ A Red Kangaroo holding food in its paws. It is using its strong tail as a prop.

5

STAYING ALERT

Kangaroos and their relatives have many enemies. These include dingos, dogs, foxes, and eagles. Kangaroos must always be alert for danger.

When a kangaroo is alert, it stands up and looks around for an attacker. It sniffs to catch a strange scent. It can turn each ear in a different direction. This helps it check all around it for strange noises.

If a kangaroo hears, sees, or smells danger, it hops away as fast as it can. Other kangaroos are warned by the movement and by the thump of its feet on the ground. The whole mob hops away fast.

◄ An alert Eastern Grey Kangaroo with one ear turned to the back and one turned to the front.

A Red-Legged Pademelon and her joey. ►
They are looking around for danger.

HOW KANGAROOS MOVE

▲ A Mareeba Rock Wallaby hopping down a steep cliff.

Hopping is the fastest and easiest way for kangaroos and wallabies to travel long distances.

They tuck their paws close to their bodies and bound along on their strong hind legs. Their long tails swing up and down behind them, balancing the tops of their bodies.

◀ A male Red Kangaroo can hop at speeds up to 34 miles per hour.

THE LARGEST AND THE SMALLEST KANGAROOS

The largest member of the kangaroo family is the Red Kangaroo. A big male Red Kangaroo will stand up to 6 feet tall and weigh 187 pounds. He will have a strong, muscular chest.

The Musky Rat Kangaroo is the smallest kangaroo relative. A big male will weigh only one pound. Unlike their large relations, Musky Rat Kangaroos build nests and eat fruit and insects.

▲ The Musky Rat Kangaroo lives in rainforests in north Queensland.   A male Red Kangaroo ▶

▲ The Eastern Grey Kangaroo lives in places where there is plenty of rain.

WHERE KANGAROOS LIVE

Australia's kangaroos and wallabies can be found in many different sorts of country.

Some kangaroos live in the hot, dry desert. Others live in forests or on grassy plains, where there is plenty to eat. Rock wallabies live on steep, rocky hills. Bettongs and potoroos need thick bushes to hide under.

▲ The Brush-Tailed Bettong lives in low scrub.

▲ The Nabarlek is a rock wallaby that lives in sandstone hills.

▲ The Bridled Nailtail Wallaby lives on dry plains.

WHAT KANGAROOS EAT

A baby kangaroo lives in its mother's pouch. Here, it gets its mother's milk to drink. Even after it leaves the pouch, it will put its head back inside to drink milk.

Most adult kangaroos and wallabies eat grass or leaves. They nip them off with their sharp front teeth. Bettongs dig up underground fungus to eat.

▲ Bettongs dig up fungus to eat.

▲ A Whiptail Wallaby joey drinking milk.

▲ An Eastern Grey shows its sharp front teeth.

A wallaby holding food in its paws ▶

14

THE DAILY DRINK

▲ Common Wallaroos are alert as they drink.

Rock wallabies live in dry places. A female rock wallaby will leave a big joey hidden in the rocks when she goes to drink. The mother may carry water back to her joey in her mouth.

Rufous Hare Wallabies can survive for a long time without drinking water. Their bodies get enough water from the plants they eat.

Some kangaroos live in very dry country. They may have to travel a long way to find water. Usually, they drink at night. They stay alert when they are drinking because there is little protection at the water's edge.

▲ An Eastern Grey Kangaroo drinking.

◄ The Red Kangaroo's ears are turned to the back, listening for any strange noises.

LIFE IN A MOB

Big kangaroos and wallabies often live in groups called mobs. A large mob may have up to 50 kangaroos in it.

Kangaroos that live in mobs are usually found in open woodlands and grassy plains.

A mob is made up of smaller groups of 5 to 10 kangaroos. Several females stay together in a small group. They will have joeys in their pouches. Older joeys will also be part of the group.

When a female in the mob is ready to mate, the biggest, strongest male mates with her. He will probably be the father of most of the joeys in the group to which the female belongs.

◄ Two male Red Kangaroos at rest. Only the strongest male will get to mate with the females of the mob.

Eastern Grey Kangaroos live in mobs. ►
The females of a mob stay together.

A KANGAROO'S DAY

▲ A Bridled Nailtail Wallaby in its day shelter.

Most kangaroos come out to feed at sunset. They spend the night eating and drinking. At dawn, they hop back to their daytime resting places.

During the day, kangaroos shelter and sleep in the shade. Some kangaroos scrape out a cool bed for themselves in the sand. The Bridled Nailtail Wallaby makes a hollow under spinifex. Here, it dozes the day away.

▲ Red Kangaroos hopping out to feed at sunset.

▲ A Western Grey Kangaroo resting during the day.

▲ Eastern Grey Kangaroos alarmed while feeding at dawn.

The male Red Kangaroo, below, has scraped a hollow in the ground. He will spend the day lying back in his cool bed, relaxing and dozing.

The female Red Kangaroo, opposite, lives in country that has had little rain. She has come out at night to find grass to eat.

COURTING

▲ A male Mareeba Rock Wallaby will sniff and lick a female to court her.

When rain makes grass and other plants grow, kangaroos and wallabies breed. A male will court a female by pawing, sniffing, and licking her. He may stay with her for two or three days before she is ready to mate with him. During this time, he may fight with other males that also want to court her.

◀ A pair of Red-Necked Wallabies and a joey.

BABY KANGAROOS

A female kangaroo has a pouch on her belly. Inside are four nipples. A tiny newborn joey climbs into the pouch and sucks milk from a nipple.

The joey stays in the pouch until it has grown fur and can keep itself warm. Then it leaves the pouch for short times to eat grass and hop around. When there is danger or if it is hungry, the joey dives back inside the pouch.

▲ A tiny joey in the pouch. It is sucking the end of one of its mother's nipples.

This Red-Necked Wallaby joey can hop back into its mother's pouch to drink from the nipple we can see in the pouch. ▶

The joey investigates some leaves, but stays ▶
near the safety of its mother.

BRINGING UP A JOEY

A joey dives into its mother's pouch head-first. It then somersaults and ends up with its head near the pouch opening. As the joey gets bigger, it stays out of the pouch for longer and longer periods of time. One day, its mother will not let it get back into her pouch. However, it will still put its head inside the pouch to drink milk.

◀ An Eastern Grey Kangaroo and her joey.

▲ A Whiptail Wallaby and her big joey.

LEARNING TO BE A KANGAROO

Finally, a young kangaroo leaves the pouch for good. Its mother will not let it drink her milk, and the joey has to eat grass and other plants. Young female kangaroos stay near their mothers for a long time. Young males wander away from their mothers' groups. It may be five years before they are big enough to court and win a mate.

A Red-Necked Wallaby and her big joey. ▶

◀ A young Eastern Grey Kangaroo

KANGAROOS FIGHTING

Two male kangaroos fight to find out who is stronger. The winner may mate with a female.

Fighting kangaroos stand tall. They use their claws to rake each other's heads and chests.

They hold each other, wrestle, and kick out with their hind legs. The stronger male may push the weaker one to the ground. A fight ends when one kangaroo gives up and hops away.

◀ Real fighting. In the wild, the loser breaks away and hops off.

▲ Play fighting. These two young wallabies are testing out their strength.

THE SMALL ONES

Potoroos, pademelons, and the Quokka are small members of the kangaroo family. Pademelons live in forests and eat grass at the forest edges. Potoroos eat insects as well as plants. The Quokka lives on Rottnest Island off the coast of Western Australia. It eats leaves.

▲ The Quokka is a leaf-eater.

▲ The Red-Necked Pademelon lives in thick forest. It eats grass at the edges of the forest.

A Long-Nosed Potoroo ▶

SOME WALLABIES AND WALLAROOS

▲ The Black Wallaroo is a wary animal.

▲ An Agile Wallaby grooming its fur.

Wallabies are small kangaroos. Some wallabies live in country that is used for sheep. However, sheep and wallabies eat different sorts of grass, so there is enough food for both.

Wallaroos live in hilly country. They have shorter hind legs than other kangaroos. They also have rough soles on their feet. These two things help them move safely and quickly on hillsides.

◄ A female Common Wallaroo in her rocky home.

A Red-necked Wallaby
and large joey

A young Whiptail
Wallaby

TWO BIG KANGAROOS

Eastern and Western Grey Kangaroos live in forests and bushland, where there is plenty of rain. A big male will weigh 154 pounds, twice as much as a female.

The Red Kangaroo lives in dry inland areas. The male Red Kangaroo is a brick-red color. Some females are red, but most are blue-grey.

▲ An Eastern Grey Kangaroo

▲ A Red Kangaroo play-fighting with a human.

A male Red Kangaroo ▶

RARE KANGAROOS

Some small kangaroos have become rare. This is because some have been killed off by foxes and cats. Others died out after the grass they fed on was eaten by rabbits, sheep, and cattle. Today, the rare ones survive only where they are protected.

▲ The Rufous Hare Wallaby is found only on two tiny islands.

◄ Bridled Nailtail Wallabies live in one small area of dry country.

Burrowing Bettongs have been ▲ killed by foxes and cats.

KANGAROOS THAT CLIMB

Rock wallabies live on rocky hills and piles of boulders. A rock wallaby can bound up or down steep slopes. The soles of its feet are rough. This helps them grip slippery rocks. The rock wallaby uses its long tail for balance.

Tree kangaroos are found in rainforests. The claws on a tree kangaroo's paws and its rough-soled feet help it to climb trees. It walks along the wider branches to get leaves to eat. It can jump to another tree or to the ground.

▲ A Yellow-Footed Rock Wallaby

▲ A young Lumholtz's Tree Kangaroo

44

A Brush-Tailed Rock Wallaby ▶

▲ This Eastern Grey Kangaroo has no fear of the car. Many kangaroos are killed on roads.

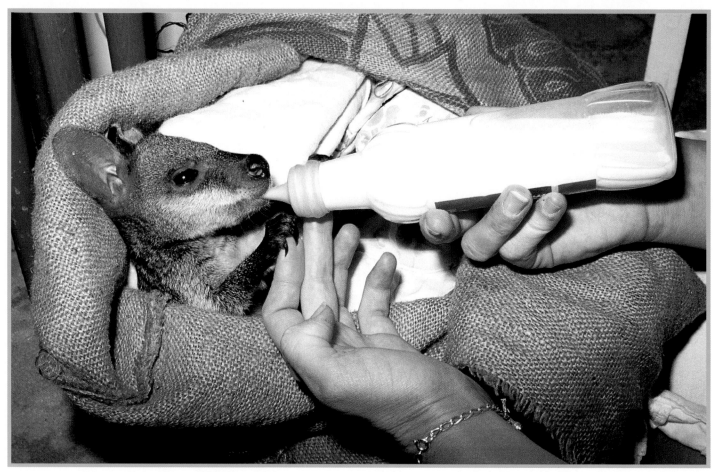

▲ A wallaby joey whose mother was killed by a car is being fostered by humans.

KANGAROOS AND PEOPLE

In the past, people hunted kangaroos for their meat and skins. Today, some kangaroos are still hunted for pet food. However, many people spend their lives working to protect and help all kangaroos.

▲ The Aboriginal people have shown kangaroos in their rock art for many thousands of years.

▲ A visitor to a sanctuary meets a mob of kangaroos.

MEETING A KANGAROO

In some places, kangaroos become used to humans. You can even touch these kangaroos.

When you meet a kangaroo, you need to move slowly and speak quietly. Then you can touch its soft fur and look into its large, dark eyes.

▲ A magic moment in the cold dawn.

◄ Meeting a kangaroo.

49

iNDEX OF ANiMALS PiCTURED

FURTHER READING & INTERNET RESOURCES

For more information on Australia's animals, check out the following books and Web sites.

Cox, Robert and Jim Robins (illustrator) The Kangaroo Who Couldn't Hop. (2000) Lothian Publishing Co.; ISBN: 0734401655

Children will love reading about this kangaroo that has problems doing what kangaroos are supposed to do and how this problem is solved.

Hewett, Joan and Richard Hewett (photographer). A Kangaroo Joey Grows Up (Baby Animals). (September 2001) Carolrhoda Books; ISBN: 0822500914

This delightful picture book shows the stages of a kangaroo joey as it grows up.

Langeland, Deidre, Frank Ordaz (illustrator), and Ranye Kaye (narrator). Kangaroo Island: The Story of an Australian Mallee Forest. (April 1998) Soundprints Corp. Audio; ISBN: 156899544X

As morning comes to Kangaroo Island following a thunderstorm, a mother kangaroo finds her lost baby, and a burned eucalyptus tree sprouts buds and becomes a new home for animals. The cassette that comes with the book adds sounds of sea lions barking, sea gulls calling, crickets humming, and even a raging forest fire.

Ratner, Susan. Kandoo Kangaroo Hops Into Homeschool. (September 2000) Master Books; ISBN: 0890512906

When a young kangaroo asks a lot of questions, her parents know it's time to homeschool. At first, school seems like a lot for a little kangaroo, but she soon learns that she "Kandoo" all sorts of things.

http://members.austarmetro.com.au/~jennt/Roo/infroo.html

This Web site has some good information on kangaroos and wallabies, including information on their height and weight, habitat, mating behaviors, life cycle, and more.

http://www.furry.org.au/kangaroos/

A great site with information on kangaroo and wallabies. Find out about kangaroo behavior, mating habits, and more, all accompanied by amazing color photos.

http://www.lincolnzoo.org/spotlight-wallaby.html

A page from The Lincoln Zoo's Web site providing a great run-down of information on a specific type of wallaby, the Red-Necked Wallaby.

http://home.mira.net/~areadman/aussie.htm

This fabulous Web site is dedicated to the creatures of Australia. It contains a comprehensive listing of the animals of Australia, with links to more in-depth information about Australia's wildlife.

http://users.orac.net.au/~mhumphry/austwild.html

This Web site has information on a few of the more "famous" members of Australia's wildlife. Read interesting facts about kangaroos, koalas, wombats, kookaburras, emus, platypuses, and echidnas.

NATURE KIDS SERIES

Birdlife
Australia is home to some of the most interesting, colorful, and noisy birds on earth. Discover some of the many different types, including parrots, kingfishers, and owls.

Frogs and Reptiles
Australia has a wide variety of environments, and there is at least one frog or reptile that calls each environment home. Discover the frogs and reptiles living in Australia.

Kangaroos and Wallabies
The kangaroo is one of the most well-known Australian creatures. Learn interesting facts about kangaroos and wallabies, a close cousin.

Marine Fish
The ocean surrounding Australia is home to all sorts of marine fish. Discover their interesting shapes, sizes, and colors, and learn about the different types of habitat in the ocean.

Rainforest Animals
Australia's rainforests are home to a wide range of animals, including snakes, birds, frogs, and wallabies. Discover a few of the creatures that call the rainforests home.

Rare & Endangered Wildlife
Animals all over the world need our help to keep from becoming extinct. Learn about the special creatures in Australia that are in danger of disappearing forever.

Sealife
Australia is surrounded by sea. As a result, there is an amazing variety of life that lives in these waters. Dolphins, crabs, reef fish, and eels are just a few of the animals highlighted in this book.

Wildlife
Australia is known for its unique creatures, such as the kangaroo and the koala. Read about these and other special creatures that call Australia home.